Let's Play JAZZ

1 *volume*

KEYBOARD

GUITAR
chord symbols

PIANO

ORGAN

BACKING TRACKS CD
full and minus one
transcriptions

arrangements
DENIS ROUX & THIERRY JAN

Carisch

album © 2000 by NUOVA CARISCH s.r.l. - Milano

THE COMPACT DISC

The pitch for tuning A is given at the beginning.
For every piece you can first listen to the complete version with melody and orchestral accompaniment, and then the version with only the accompaniment, which you can play along with.

THE PARTS

For every piece you will find three versions:
- a simplified version: with the melody in the right hand and an easy accompanying line in the left hand (for beginners)
- a version for organ: with the melody in the right hand, chords in the left, and bass-line for the pedal.
- a version for solo piano: for use with piano or keyboard (medium difficulty)

VOICE

It is possible to use the versions contained in the CD for singing the pieces. The texts are found in the sheets inserted at the end of the volume and the melodies are given in the keyboard parts (right hand).

GUITAR

All of the guitar boxes for the chords are given in the single sheets inserted at the end of the volume. The sheet for each piece contains, besides the guitar chords, the text and a table with the complete harmonies, measure by measure. The melodies can also be played on the guitar using the melodic line (right hand) of the keyboard versions.

OTHER INSTRUMENTS

It is also possible to play the melody parts or to improvise with other instruments such as flute, violin, etc. It should be noted that for instruments such as the clarinet or the saxophone the melodies will have to be transposed. A bass can be added to the group, playing from the pedal part of the organ versions.

CONTENTS

IN THE MOOD

Music by J. Garland

Easy Piano

Thème

⊕ 3ᵉ fois al Coda

1

2

%

⊕ CODA

IN THE MOOD

Music by J. Garland

Piano, Keyboard

Track 2/3

INTRODUCTION

Thème

3ᵉ fois al Coda

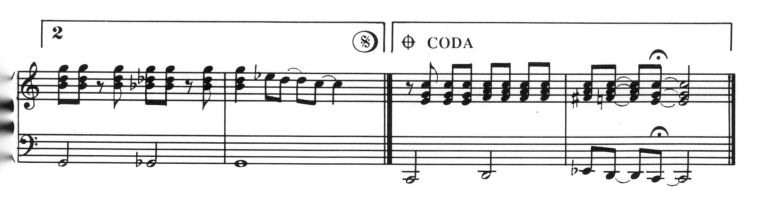

IN THE MOOD

Music by J. Garland

Organ

MOONLIGHT SERENADE

Words and Music by Glenn Miller & Mitchell Parish

Easy Piano

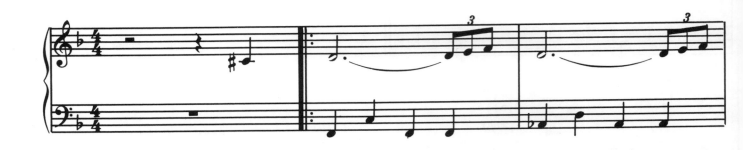

Pour finir

13

MOONLIGHT SERENADE

Words and Music by Glenn Miller & Mitchell Parish

Piano, Keyboard

Pour
finir

MOONLIGHT SERENADE

Words and Music by Glenn Miller & Mitchell Parish

Organ

FLY ME TO THE MOON

Words and Music by B. Howard

Easy Piano

© 1934 by Hampshire House Publ. Corp. New York, N.Y., USA

Sub-Editore per l'Italia: Edizioni Musicali MARIO AROMANDO s.r.l. - Galleria del Corso, 4 - 20122 Milano

FLY ME TO THE MOON

Words and Music by B. Howard

Piano, Keyboard

FLY ME TO THE MOON

Words and Music by B. Howard

Organ

NIGHT AND DAY

Words and music by Cole Porter

Easy Piano

NIGHT AND DAY

Words and music by Cole Porter

Piano, Keyboard

Track 8/9

NIGHT AND DAY

Words and music by Cole Porter

Organ

SAMBA DE UMA NOTA SO

Words by N.Mendonça - Music by A.C.Jobim

Easy Piano

SAMBA DE UMA NOTA SO

Words by N.Mendonça - Music by A.C.Jobim

Piano, Keyboard

SAMBA DE UMA NOTA SO

Words by N.Mendonça - Music by A.C.Jobim

Organ

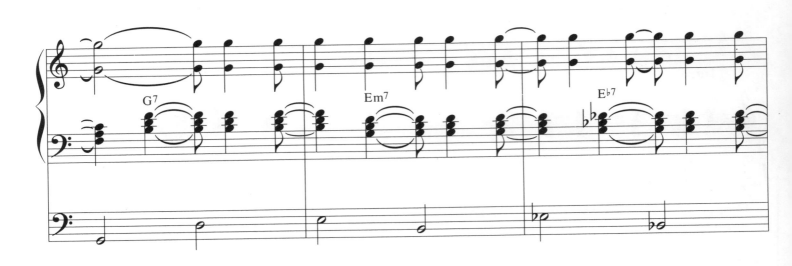

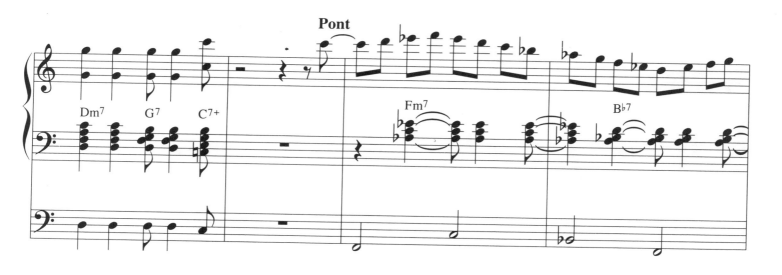

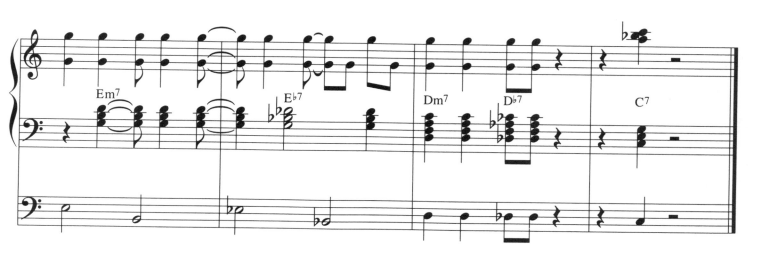

ROSES OF PICARDY

Words by Frederick E. Weatherly - Music by Haydn Wood

Easy Piano

ROSES OF PICARDY

Words by Frederick E. Weatherly - Music by Haydn Wood

Piano, Keyboard

Track 12/13

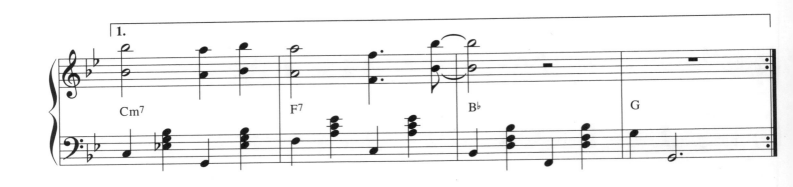

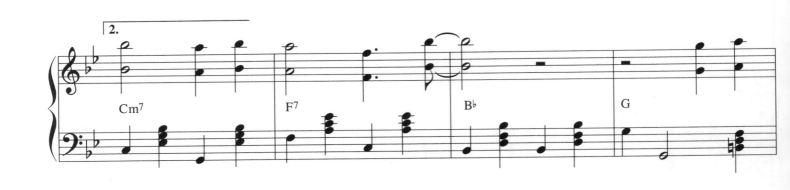

ROSES OF PICARDY

Words by Frederick E. Weatherly - Music by Haydn Wood

Organ

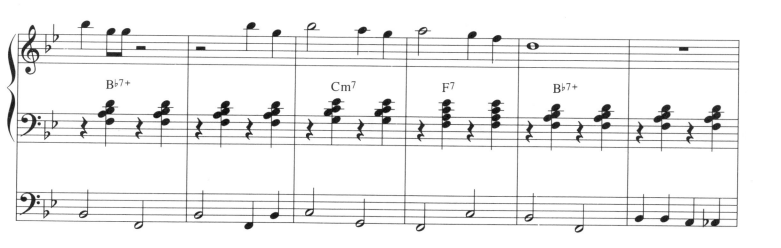

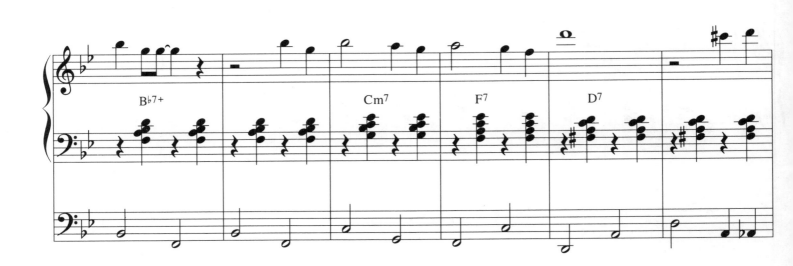

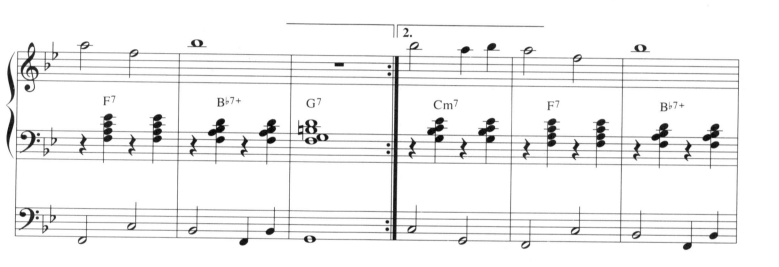

CRY ME A RIVER

Words and Music by Arthur Hamilton

Easy Piano

Intro

Thème

CRY ME A RIVER

Words and Music by Arthur Hamilton

Piano, Keyboard

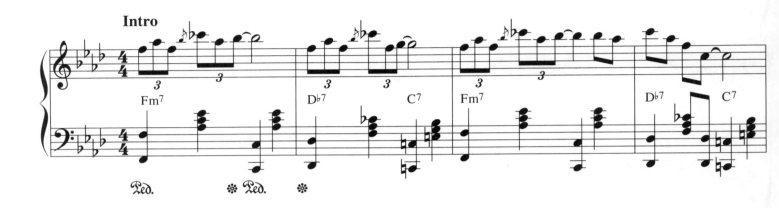

CRY ME A RIVER

Words and Music by Arthur Hamilton

Organ

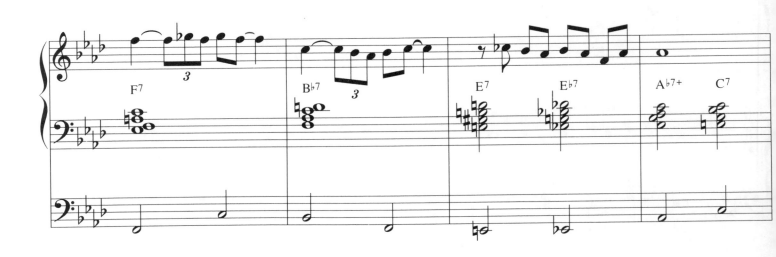

LES FEUILLES MORTES

Words by J. Prévert - Music by J. Kosma

Organ

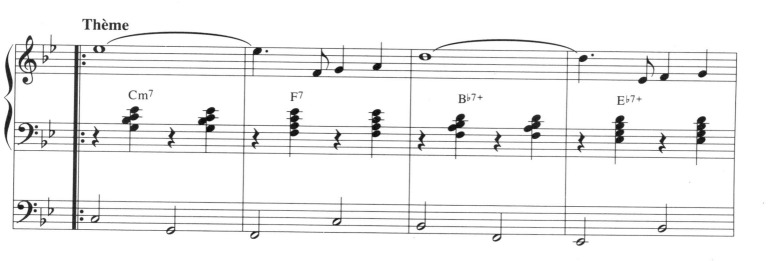

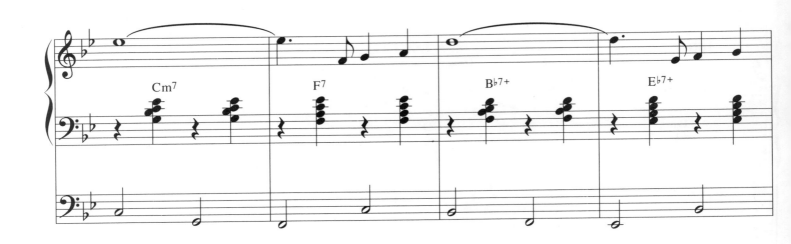

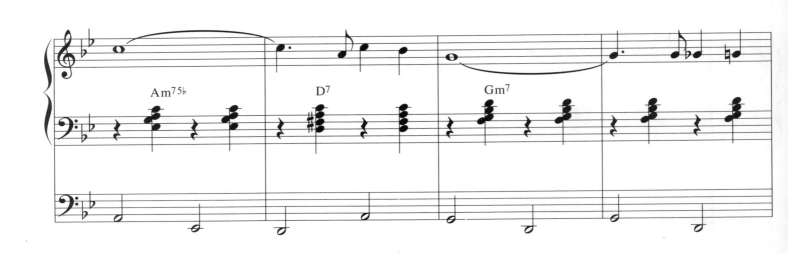

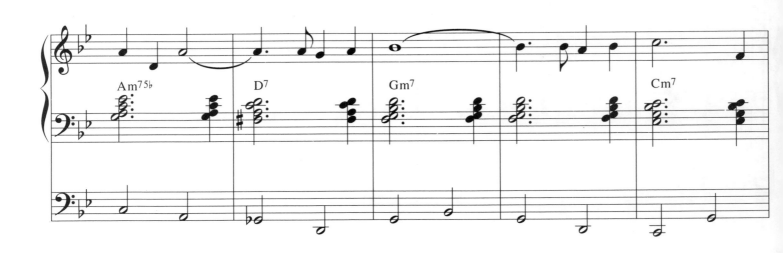

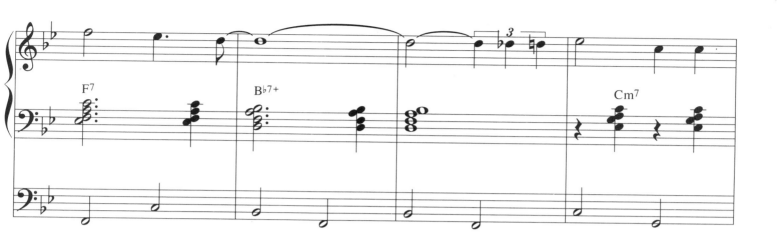

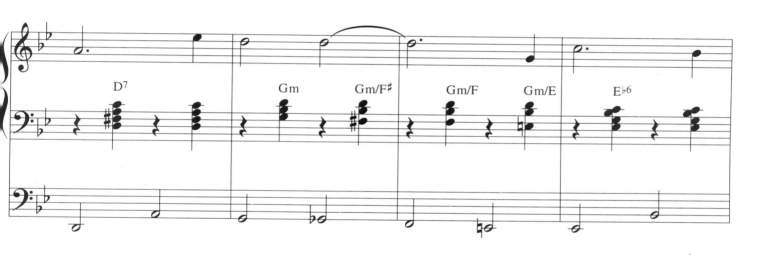

LES FEUILLES MORTES

Words by J.Prévert - Music by J.Kosma

Easy Piano

LES FEUILLES MORTES

Words by J.Prévert - Music by J.Kosma

Piano, Keyboard

IN THE MOOD

harmonic table

$\frac{4}{4}$	**4**	D7/9	./.	G7/9	./.	𝄋 C13	./.
	C13	./.	F7/9	./.	C13	./.	G7/9
	G7/9	3° to CODA ⊕ ./.	C / Dm7	D♯° / C · Dm7	𝄋 C7/9	F7/9	C7/9
	F7/9	C7/9	F7/9	⌐1°⌐ G7 / G°	G7/9 ·	⌐2°⌐ G7 / G°	G7/9 𝄋
CODA ⊕	C / Dm7	D♯° / C Dm7					

guitar chords

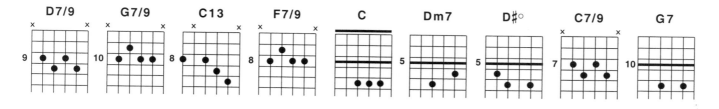

D7/9   G7/9   C13   F7/9   C   Dm7   D♯°   C7/9   G7

G°

lyrics

Mister what chacallum, what cha doin' tonight?
Hope you're in the mood, because I'm feelin' just right
How's about a corner with a table for two
Where the music's mellow in some gay rendez-vous?
There's no chance romancin' with a blue attitude
You've got to do some dancin' to get in the mood

Sister what chacallum, that's a timely idea
Something swing adila would be good to my hear
Ev'rybody must agree that dancin' has charms
When you have that certain one you love in your arms
Steppin' out with you will be a sweet interlude
A builder upper that will put me in the mood

In the mood, that's it, I've got it
In the mood, your ear will spot it
In the mood, oh what a hot hit
Be alive and get the jive
You've got to learn how: hep hep hep
Hep like a hepper, pep pep pep
Hot as a pepper, step step step
Step like a stepper, we're muggin' and huggin'
We're in the mood

MOONLIGHT SERENADE

harmonic table

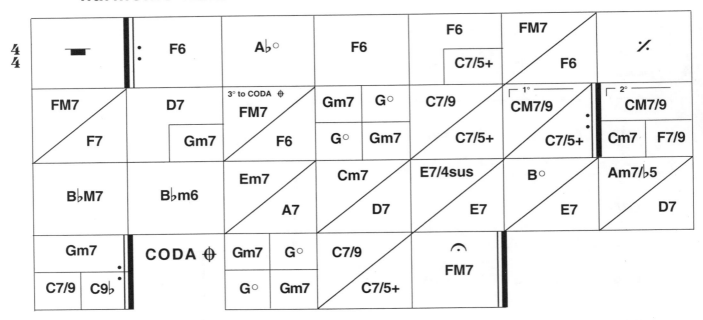

guitar chords

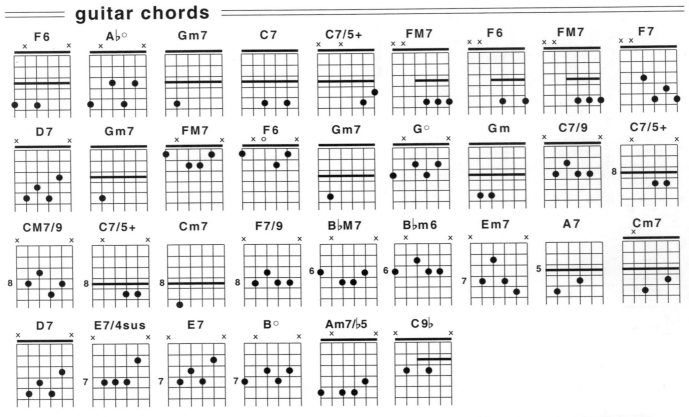

lyrics

I stand at your gate and the song that I sing
Is of Moonlight
I stand and I wait for the touch of your hand
In the June night
The roses are sighing a moonlight serenade
The stars are a glow and tonight how their light
Sets me dreaming
My love, do you know that your eyes are like stars
Brigthly beaming?
I bring you and sing you a moonlight serenade

Let us stray till break of day in love's
"Valley of dreams"
Just you and I, a summer sky a heavenly breeze
Kissing the trees
So don't let me wait, come to me tenderly
In the June night
I stand at your gate and I sing you a song
In the moonlight
A love song my darling, a moonlight serenade

FLY ME TO THE MOON

harmonic table

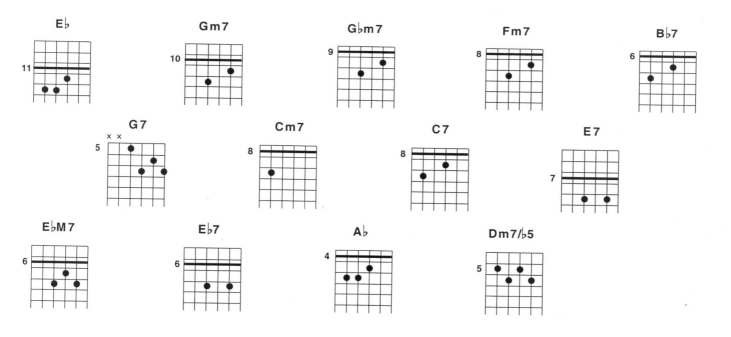

guitar chords

lyrics

Fly me to the moon, and let me play among the stars
Let me see what spring is like on Jupiter and Mars
In other words hold my hand
In other words darling kiss me

Fill my heart with song and let me sing forever more
You are all I long for all I worship and adore
In other words please be true
In other words I love you

NIGHT AND DAY

harmonic table

$\frac{4}{4}$: Dm7/♭5	G7	CM7	∕.	Dm7/♭5	G7	CM7	∕.
F♯m7/♭5	Fm7	Em7	E♭°	Dm7	G7	CM7	1° ∕. :
CM7	E♭M7	∕.	CM7	∕.	E♭M7	∕.	CM7
CM7	F♯m7/♭5	Fm7	Em7	E♭°	Dm7	G7	CM7 2° al CODA ⊕ : ∕.
CODA ⊕	G7	CM7	∕.	B♭M7	∕.	▬	CM7

guitar chords

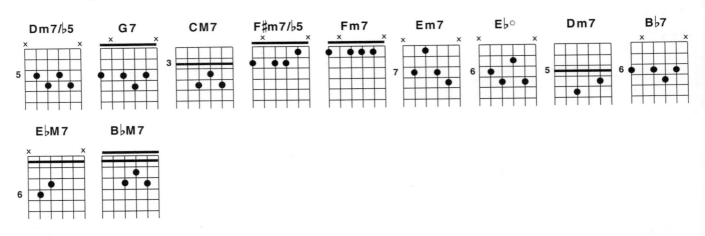

Dm7/♭5   G7   CM7   F♯m7/♭5   Fm7   Em7   E♭°   Dm7   B♭7

E♭M7   B♭M7

lyrics

Like the beat, beat, beat, of the tom-tom,
when the jungle shadows fall,
Like the tick, tick, tock of the stately clock,
as it stand against the wall
Like the drip, drip, drip, of the raindrops,
when the summer show'r is through;
So a voice within me keeps repeating, you, you, you,
Night and Day
You are the one, only you under the moon
and under the sun.
Whether near to me or far,
It's no matter, darling, when you are, I think of you
Night and Day, day and night.

Why is it so, that this longing for you follows wherever I go?
In the roaring traffic's boom,
In the silence of my lonely room, I think of you
Night and Day, Night and Day
Under the hide of me there's an
Oh, such a hungry yearning, burning inside of me.
And it's torment won't be through
'Til you let me spend my life making love to you,
Day and night,
Night and Day...

SAMBA DE UMA NOTA SO

harmonic table

Intro Dm7 / Db7	CM7	Dm7 / Db7	CM7	Dm7 / Db7	CM7	Dm7 / G7
CM7	**A Theme** Em7	Eb7	Dm7	Db7/5-	Gm7/11	C7/5-
F7+	Bb7/9	Em7	Eb7	Dm7 / Db7/5-	C6/9	**B** Fm7
Bb13	EbM7/9	./.	Ebm7	Ab13	DbM7/9	Dm7/5- / Dbm7/5-
C Em7	Eb7	Dm7 / Db7/5	C6/9			

A.B.A.A.B.A.C.

guitar chords

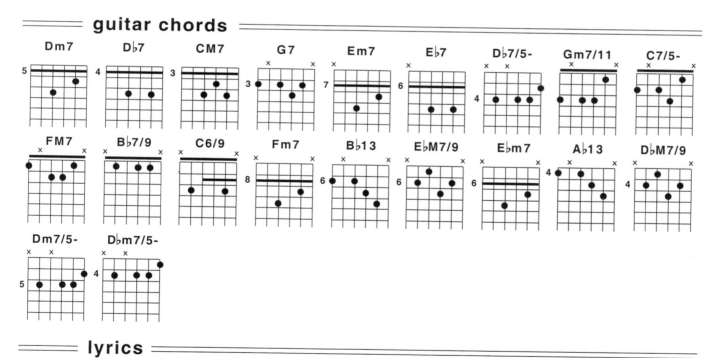

lyrics

Eis aqui este sambinha feita numa nota so
Outras notas va o entrar mas a base é uma so
Esta outra é consequència do que a cabo de dizer
Como en su a consequència ine vita vel de você.

Quanta gente existe par ai que fala tanto e nao diz nada,
ou que se nada
ja meu tilisei de toda aes cala e no final nao sobrou nada
nao deu em nada

E voltei pra minha nota camo eu votto pra você
Vou contar como minha nota camo eu gosto de você
E quem quer todas as notas
Re mi fa sol la si do
Ficu sempre sem nenhuma
Fique numa nota so.

ROSES OF PICARDY

harmonic table

Intro							
Cm7	F7	B♭	∕.	Cm7	F7	B♭M7 ▷	G7/5+
Theme Cm7	F7	*B♭M7	∕.	*Cm7	F7/9	*B♭M7	1° *B♭M7 / A7 · A♭7
G7	∕.	Cm7	∕.	C7	C7/9	F7	∕.
2° D7	∕.	G7	∕.	C7	C7/9	Cm7	F7
B♭M7	G7	G7	F7	*B♭	*B♭		

guitar chords

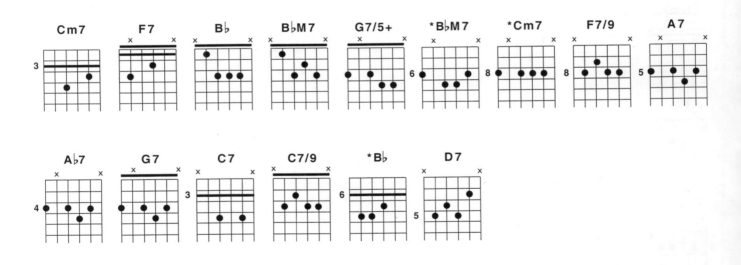

Cm7 · F7 · B♭ · B♭M7 · G7/5+ · *B♭M7 · *Cm7 · F7/9 · A7
A♭7 · G7 · C7 · C7/9 · *B♭ · D7

lyrics

Roses are shining in Picardy
in the hush of the silver dew.
Roses are flow'ring in Picardy,
but there's never a rose like you!
And the roses will die with the summertime,
and our roads may be far a part.
But there's one rose that dies not in Picardy!
'Tis the rose that I keep in my Heart!

Roses are shining in Picardy,
in the hush of the silver dew.
Roses are flow'ring in Picardy,
but there's never a rose like you!
And the roses will die with the summertime,
and our roads may be far a part.
But there's one rose that dies not in Picardy!
'Tis the rose that I keep in my Heart!

CRY ME A RIVER

harmonic table

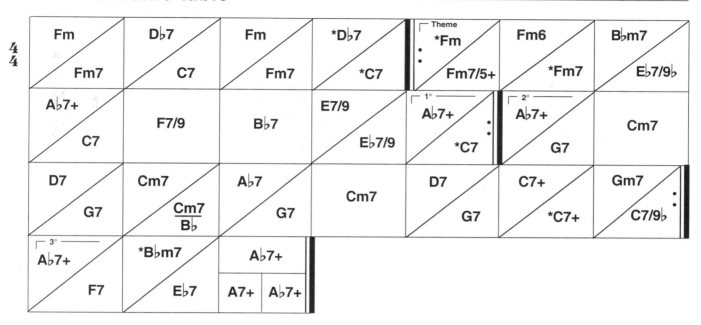

guitar chords

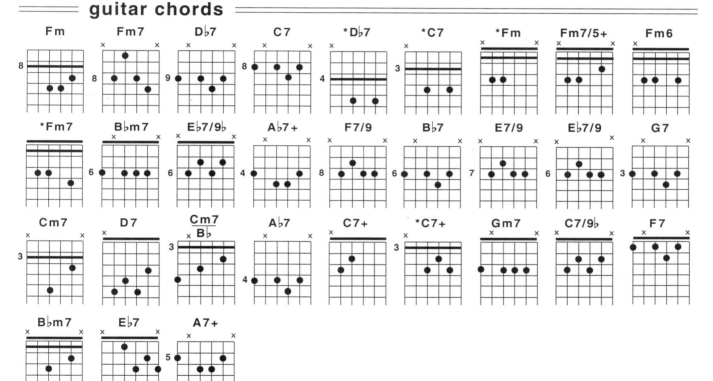

lyrics

Now, you say you're lonely, you cry the long night thru;
Well, you can cry me a river, cry me a river,
I cried a river over you
Now, you say you're sorry, for bein' so untrue;
Well, you can cry me a river, cry me a river,
I cried a river over you

You drove me, nearly drove me out of my head,
While you never shed a tear.
Remember? I remember all that you said;

Told me love was too plebelan,
told me you were thru with me, an

Now, you say you love me, well, just to prove you do
Com'on an' cry me a river, cry me a river,
I cried a river over you

LES FEUILLES MORTES

harmonic table

$\frac{4}{4}$

Intro Gm7	Am7/♭5 / D7/♭9	Gm7	D7 ▷	‖: Cm7	F7/9 / F7/♭9	B♭M7
E♭M7	Am7/♭5	⌐1° D7/♭9	Gm7	*Gm7 :‖	⌐2° D7/♭9	Gm7
Gm7	Am7/♭5	D7/♭9	Gm7	*Gm7	Cm7	F7/9 / F7/♭9
B♭M7	∕.	Am7/♭5	D7/♭9	Gm7 / G♭7	Fm7 / E7	E♭M7
D7/♭9	Gm7	*Gm7 ▷ ‖				

guitar chords

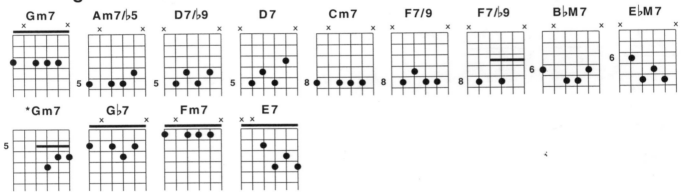

Gm7 Am7/♭5 D7/♭9 D7 Cm7 F7/9 F7/♭9 B♭M7 E♭M7
*Gm7 G♭7 Fm7 E7

lyrics

Oh! je voudrais tant que tu te souviennes
des jours hereux où nous étions amis.
En ce temps là la vie était plus belle,
et le soleil plus brûlant qu'aujourd'hui.
Les feuilles mortes se ramassent à la pelle.
Tu vois, je n'ai pas oublié.
Les feuilles mortes se ramassent à la pelle,
les souvenirs et les regrets aussi.
Et le vent du Nord les emporte
dans la nuit froide de l'oubli.
Tu vois, je n'ai pas oublié la chanson que tu me chantais.

C'est une chanson qui nous ressemble,
toi tu m'amais, et je t'aimais.
Et nous vivions tous deux ensemble
toi qui m'aimais, moi qui t'aimais.
Mais la vie sépare ceux qui s'aiment,
tout doucement, sans faire de bruit.
Et la mer efface sur la sable, les pas des amants désunis.

C'est une chanson qui nous ressemble,
toi tu m'amais, et je t'aimais.
Et nous vivions tous deux ensemble
toi qui m'aimais, moi qui t'aimais.
Mais la vie sépare ceux qui s'aiment,
tout doucement, sans faire de bruit.
Et la mer efface sur la sable, les pas des amants désunis.
Les feuilles mortes se ramassent à la pelle,
les souvenirs et les regrets aussi.
Mais mon amour silencieux et fidèle
sourit toujours et remercie la vie.
Je t'amais tant, tu étais si jolie;
comment voeux tu que je t'oublie.
En ce temp là la vie etait plus belle,
et le soleil plus brûlant qu'aujourd'hui.
Tu étais ma plus douce amie...
Mais je n'ai que faire des regrets.
Et la chanson que tu chantais toujours,
toujours je l'entendrai!

INGRAF s.r.l. - Via Monte S. Genesio 7 - Milano
Stampato in Italia - Printed in Italy - Imprimé en Italie 2001

ALSO AVAILABLE

SAXOPHONE

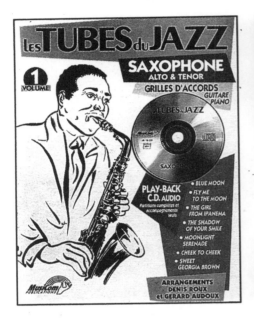  

KEYBOARD